To Heather Gail
my dearest daughter:
wishing you a
Happy Christmas
and a very
Happy New year:
(With much) Shelagh Sidery:
love:) Christmas 2000

THE FOUR SEASONS

A TREASURY OF
SEASONAL VERSE AND PROSE
SCENTED BY PENHALIGON'S

THE FOUR SEASONS

Edited by
Sheila Pickles

PAVILION

The Human Seasons

Four seasons fill the measure of the year;
There are four seasons in the mind of man;
He has his lusty Spring, when fancy clear
Takes in all beauty with an easy span;
He has his Summer, when luxuriously
Spring's honeyed cud of youthful thought he loves
To ruminate, and by such dreaming high
Is nearest unto heaven; quiet coves
His soul has in its Autumn, when his wings
He furleth close; contented so to look
On mists in idleness – to let fair things
Pass by unheeded as a threshold brook.
He has his Winter, too, of pale misfeature,
Or else he would forego his mortal nature.

John Keats 1795–1821

INTRODUCTION

Dear Reader,

The unfolding of the seasons has always seemed to me to be the great glory of the English countryside. Consistently each year nature fulfills our expectations and we welcome the return of familiar landscapes like old friends. It is mid-winter when the snowdrop triumphs through the snow, and nothing raises my spirits quite so much as seeing the crocus, boasting her bright colours, appearing in our parks and knowing that spring is on the way. After a subdued winter palette, the primary colours of spring are a feast for the eye and entice us outdoors. But having made our plans and sown our seeds we quickly tire of our overcoats, and I soon long for the hot lazy days of summer, the buzzing of the bees and the more subtle pastel colours of the lavender beds and the herbaceous borders. Summer ends for me with haymaking and the harvest festival and when we return from our summer holidays there is always an early morning chill in the air.

In the Autumn we reap the benefit of our labour in the orchard and colour once again has a large part to play. The trees turn the colour of their leaves before letting them fall and the smell of bonfires warns us of the approaching winter. This is the season of rest when the land has a peaceful and serene beauty and the weather turns us indoors. But underneath the earth the seasonal cycle continues, for when she is ready, no matter what the weather-man says, the snowdrop will appear.

To add to your enjoyment whilst reading the book, I have scented the endpapers with Penhaligon's 'Gardenia'. It is an intoxicating scent which I hope will remind you of summer all year long.

Sheila Pickles, Canonbury 1994.

SPRING

Nothing is so beautiful as spring –
When weeds, in wheels, shoot long and lovely and lush;
Thrush's eggs look little low heavens, and thrush
Through the echoing timber does so rinse and wring
The ear, it strikes like lightnings to hear him sing.

Gerard Manley Hopkins

MAIDEN MAY

MAIDEN May sat in her bower,
In her blush rose bower in flower,
Sweet of scent;
Sat and dreamed away an hour,
Half content, half uncontent.

'Why should rose blossoms be born,
Tender blossoms, on a thorn
Tho' so sweet?
Never a thorn besets the corn
Scentless in its strength complete.

'Why are roses all so frail,
At the mercy of a gale,
Of a breath?
Yet so sweet and perfect pale,
Still so sweet in life and death.'

Maiden May sat in her bower,
In her blush rose bower in flower,
Where a linnet
Made one bristling branch the tower
For her nest and young ones in it.

Christina Rossetti, 1830-1894

COWSLIPS

I THINK there is no scent on earth to come up to that of the cowslips; I fancy primroses are sickly, but cowslips are the very embodiment of spring and I do not like to see them made into wine and puddings as they are in these parts of England. A cowslip pudding sounds ideal, but it is mostly suet and imagination. Now a cowslip ball is a delight and Marjorie naturally has her fill of the sweet and dainty things. She never sees them faded or dead as long as the flowers last, for when she is in bed to-day's balls are neatly cremated; we tell her the fairies called for them for their children and the next day's balls are always fresh. I think if I were ninety I should feel young making a cowslip ball, and if Marjorie and Steeple and the cowslips were combined I could not recollect my age, of that I am sure.

From *Leaves of a Garden* by Miss Panton, c. 1910

THE WEATHER OF NEW ENGLAND

*G*ENTLEMEN: I reverently believe that the Maker who made us all, makes everything in New England – but the weather. I don't know who makes that, but I think it must be raw apprentices in the Weather Clerk's factory, who experiment and learn how in New England, for board and clothes, and then are promoted to make weather for countries that require a good article, and will take their custom elsewhere if they don't get it. There is a sumptuous variety about the New England weather that compels the stranger's admiration – and regret. The weather is always doing something there; always attending strictly to business; always getting up new designs and trying them on the people to see how they will go. But it gets through more business in spring than in any other season. In the spring I have counted one hundred and thirty six different kinds of weather inside of four and twenty hours. It was I that made the fame and fortune of that man that had that marvelous collection of weather on exhibition at the Centennial that so astounded the foreigners. He was going to travel all over the world and get specimens from all the climes. I said, 'Don't you do it; you come to New England on a favorable spring day.' I told him what we could do, in the way of style, variety, and quantity. Well, he came, and he made his collection in four days. As to variety – why, he confessed that he got hundreds of kinds of weather that he had never heard of before. And as to quantity – well, after he had picked out and discarded all that was blemished in any way, he not only had weather enough, but weather to spare; weather to hire out; weather to sell; to deposit; weather to invest; weather to give to the poor.

The people of New England are by nature patient and forbearing; but there are some things which they will not stand. Every year they kill a lot of poets for writing about 'Beautiful Spring.' These are generally casual visitors, who bring their notions of spring from somewhere else, and cannot, of course, know how the natives feel about spring. And so, the first thing they know, the opportunity to inquire how they feel has permanently gone by.

From *Annual Dinner Speech to New England Society of New York* by Mark Twain, 1835-1910

AUBADE

Hark! hark! the lark at heaven's gate sings,
And Phœbus 'gins arise,
His steeds to water at those springs
On chaliced flowers that lies;
And winking Mary-buds begin
To ope their golden eyes:
With everything that pretty bin,
My lady sweet, arise!
Arise, arise!

William Shakespeare, 1564-1616

Luncheon On The Grass

*M*Y lord has ordered the char-a-banc, and is going to drive us all to Chart, where we will lunch,' said Lady St. Jerome; ''tis a curious place, and was planted only seventy years ago by my Lord's grandfather, entirely with spruce firs, but with so much care and skill, giving each plant and tree ample distance, that they have risen to the noblest proportions, with all their green branches far-spreading on the ground like huge fans.'

It was only a drive of three or four miles entirely in the park. This was a district that had been added to the ancient enclosure; a striking scene. It was a forest of firs, but quite unlike such as might be met with in the north of Europe or of America. Every tree was perfect, huge and complete, and full of massy grace. Nothing else was permitted to grow there except juniper, of which there were abounding and wondrous groups, green and spiral; the whole contrasting with the tall brown fern of which there were quantities about cut for the deer.

The turf was dry and mossy, and the air pleasant. It was a balmy day. They sat down by the great trees, the servants opened the luncheon baskets, which were a present from Balmoral. Lady St. Jerome was seldom seen to greater advantage than distributing her viands under such circumstances. Never was such gay and graceful hospitality. Lothair was quite fascinated as she playfully thrust a paper of lobster-sandwiches into his hand, and enjoined Monsignore Catesby to fill his tumbler with Chablis.

From *Lothair* by Benjamin Disraeli, 1804-1881

THE TWENTY-SECOND OF
FEBRUARY, 1940

*T*HE hard weather has gone for the moment, and the first deceptive day of Spring arrived with so warm a rush as to make us believe it would be succeeded by many others. Of course with our reason we know that this is unlikely. We know that a bit of February is still to come and the whole of March, frequently one of the most unpleasant months in the calendar. Yet it is difficult to be prudent and sceptical when the first sunlight one has seen for many weeks wakes one between the curtains and makes one leap from bed to find a very different kind of day awaiting one outside. Warm air is surprising after the shivering cold one has learned to expect. It is surprising to find that one wants to throw off one's coat instead of dragging it closely round one. How delightful to be free of the heavy coat! How delightful to walk unhampered, even if only for one day! How delightful to enjoy in a platitudinous way the simple pleasures of the first suggestion of spring: the birds singing once more, the earth soft to the tread after the stiffness of frost, the evidence of things beginning again to love and bud and grow.

We Britons are perhaps specially sensitive to such movements of the seasons, since our seasons melt and merge into one another more elastically than the more violently demarcated seasons of stronger climates. Our seasons interchange their character in a way unknown to the extremes of North or South. Thus the citizen of Leningrad knows that the spring will not arrive till the middle of May and arranges his existence and his mind to suit that necessity; he does not expect the spring and so is not disappointed when he does not get it somewhere in the middle of February; the inhabitant of Shiraz, on the other hand, would be extremely indignant if his spring suddenly reverted to winter. We have learnt to be more tolerant. We are grateful for the one warm day coming in the midst of our tribulations, and with our usual happy-go-lucky optimism assume at once that the warm happy days have arrived to last.

From *Country Notes in Wartime* by Vita Sackville-West, 1892-1962

SPRING

WHEN daisies pied and violets blue,
And lady-smocks all silver-white,
And cuckoo-buds of yellow hue
Do paint the meadows with delight,
The cuckoo then, on every tree,
Mocks married men; for thus sings he,
Cuckoo!
Cuckoo, cuckoo! – O word of fear,
Unpleasing to a married ear!

When shepherds pipe on oaten straws,
And merry larks are ploughmen's clocks,
When turtles tread, and rooks, and daws,
And maidens bleach their summer smocks
The cuckoo then, on every tree,
Mocks married men; for thus sings he,
Cuckoo!
Cuckoo, cuckoo! – O word of fear,
Unpleasing to a married ear!

William Shakespeare, 1564-1616

A Spring Resolution

*I*T was now early spring – the time of going to grass with the sheep, when they have the first feed of the meadows, before these are laid up for mowing. The winds, which had been blowing east for several weeks, had veered to the southward, and the middle of spring had come abruptly – almost without a beginning. It was that period in the vernal quarter when we may suppose the Dryads to be waking for the season. The vegetable world begins to move and swell and the saps to rise, till in the completest silence of lone gardens and trackless plantations, where everything seems helpless and still after the bond and slavery of frost, there are bustlings, strainings, united thrusts, and pulls-all-together, in comparison with which the powerful tugs of cranes and pulleys in a noisy city are but pigmy-efforts.

Boldwood, looking into the distant meadows, saw there three figures. They were those of Miss Everdene, Shepherd Oak, and Cainy Ball.

When Bathsheba's figure shone upon the farmer's eyes it lighted him up as the moon lights up a great tower. A man's body is as the shell, or the tablet, of his soul, as he is reserved or ingenuous, overflowing or self-contained. There was a change in Boldwood's exterior from its former impassibleness; and his face showed that he was now living outside his defences for the first time, and with a fearful sense of exposure. It is the usual experience of strong natures when they love.

At last he arrived at a conclusion. It was to go across and inquire boldly of her.

From *Far From the Madding Crowd* by Thomas Hardy, 1840-1928

TO SPRING

O THOU with dewy locks, who lookest down
Through the clear windows of the morning, turn
Thine angel eyes upon our western isle,
Which in full choir hails thy approach, O Spring!

The hills tell one another, and the listening
Valleys hear; all our longing eyes are turn'd
Up to thy bright pavilions: issue forth
And let thy holy feet visit our clime!

Come o'er the eastern hills, and let our winds
Kiss thy perfumèd garments; let us taste
Thy morn and evening breath; scatter thy pearls
Upon our lovesick land that mourns for thee.

O deck her forth with thy fair fingers; pour
Thy soft kisses on her bosom; and put
Thy golden crown upon her languish'd head,
Whose modest tresses are bound up for thee.

William Blake, 1757-1827

APRIL À LA MODE

*Y*OUNG girls, but only young girls, have entirely discarded long dresses for dancing. Long dresses, however, are still worn by ladies, who do not dance – or, at the utmost, dance in quadrilles, when the long dress, if well worn, is more graceful than short skirts. With short dresses, laced-up shoes, as high as Polish boots, are invariably worn.

Ball dresses are made of almost every material, of every colour, and style. Everything is allowed, so long as it looks pretty, and is becoming to the wearer. Fashion has now but one aim, that of making every lady look her best, whatever her complexion, features, or figure may be. Thus, velvet may be mixed with satin, silk, brocade, tulle and gauze, or each may be worn by itself. This liberty of colour and material, allows a past season's dress to be renewed.

From *Parisian Gossip, The Lady's Treasury*, 1880

HOME-THOUGHTS,
FROM ABROAD

O TO be in England
Now that April's there,
And whoever wakes in England
Sees, some morning, unaware,
That the lowest boughs and the brushwood sheaf
Round the elm-tree bole are in tiny leaf,
While the chaffinch sings on the orchard bough
In England – now!

And after April, when May follows,
And the whitethroat builds, and all the swallows!
Hark, where my blossom'd pear-tree in the hedge
Leans to the field and scatters on the clover
Blossoms and dewdrops – at the bent spray's edge –
That's the wise thrush; he sings each song twice over,

Lest you should think he never could recapture
The first fine careless rapture!
And though the fields look rough with hoary dew,
All will be gay when noontide wakes anew
The buttercups, the little children's dower
– Far brighter than this gaudy melon-flower!

Robert Browning, 1812-1889

SUMMER

Great is the sun and wide he goes
Through empty heaven without repose
And in the blue and glowing days
More thick than rain he showers his rays!

Robert Louis Stevenson

SONNET

SHALL I compare thee to a summer's day?
Thou art more lovely and more temperate.
Rough winds do shake the darling buds of May,
And summer's lease hath all too short a date:
Sometime too hot the eye of heaven shines,
And often is his gold complexion dimm'd;
And every fair from fair some time declines,
By chance, or nature's changing course, untrimm'd;
But thy eternal summer shall not fade
Nor lose possession of that fair thou ow'st;
Nor shall Death brag thou wand'rest in his shade,
When in eternal lines to time thou grow'st.
So long as men can breathe or eyes can see,
So long lives this, and this gives life to thee.

William Shakespeare, 1564-1616

An Absent Lover Returns

Molly was sitting in her pretty white invalid's dress, half reading, half dreaming, for the June air was so clear and ambient, the garden so full of bloom, the trees so full of leaf, that reading by the open window was only a pretence at such a time; besides which, Mrs Gibson continually interrupted her with remarks about the pattern of her worsted work. It was after lunch – orthodox calling time, when Maria ushered in Mr Roger Hamley. Molly started up; and then stood shyly and quietly in her place while a bronzed, bearded, grave man came into the room, in whom she at first had to seek for the merry boyish face she knew by heart only two years ago. But months in the climates in which Roger had been travelling age as much as years in more temperate regions. And constant thought and anxiety, while in daily peril of life, deepen the lines of character upon the face. Moreover, the circumstances that had of late affected him personally were not of a nature to make him either buoyant or cheerful. But his voice was the same; that was the first point of the old friend Molly caught, when he addressed her in a tone far softer than he used in speaking conventional politenesses to her step-mother.

'I was so sorry to hear how ill you had been! You are looking but delicate!' letting his eyes rest upon her face with affectionate examination. Molly felt herself colour all over with the consciousness of his regard. To do something to put an end to it, she looked up, and showed him her beautiful soft grey eyes, which he never remembered to have noticed before. She smiled at him as she blushed still deeper, and said:

'Oh! I am quite strong now to what I was. It would be a shame to be ill when everything is in its full summer beauty.'

From *Wives and Daughters* by Elizabeth Gaskell, 1810-1865

AN AROMATIC JUNE

THERE had never been such a June in Eagle Country. Usually it was a month of moods, with abrupt alternations of belated frost and midsummer heat; this year, day followed day in a sequence of temperate beauty. Every morning a breeze blew steadily from the hills. Toward noon it built up great canopies of white cloud that threw a cool shadow over fields and woods; then before sunset the clouds dissolved again, and the western light rained its unobstructed brightness on the valley.

On such an afternoon Charity Royall lay on a ridge above a sunlit valley, her face pressed to the earth and the warm currents of the grass running through her. Directly in her line of vision a blackberry branch laid its frail white flowers and blue-green leaves against the sky. Just beyond, a tuft of sweet-fern uncurled between the beaded shoots of the grass, and a small yellow butterfly vibrated over them like a fleck of sunshine. This was all she saw; but she felt, above her and about her, the strong growth of the beeches clothing the ridge, the rounding of pale green cones on countless spruce branches, the push of myriads of sweet-fern fronds in the cracks of the stony slope below the wood, and the crowding shoots of meadowsweet and yellow flags in the pasture beyond. All this bubbling of sap and slipping of sheaths and bursting of calyxes was carried to her on mingled currents of fragrance. Every leaf and bud and blade seemed to contribute its exhalation to the pervading sweetness in which the pungency of pine-sap prevailed over the spice of thyme and the subtle perfume of fern, and all were merged in a moist earth-smell that was like the breath of some huge sun-warmed animal.

From *Summer* by Edith Wharton 1862-1937

ODE TO A NIGHTINGALE

My heart aches, and a drowsy numbness pains
My sense, as though of hemlock I had drunk,
 Or emptied some dull opiate to the drains
One minute past, and Lethe-wards had sunk:
 'Tis not through envy of thy happy lot,
 But being too happy in thy happiness, –
 That thou, light-winged Dryad of the trees,
 In some melodious plot
Of beechen green, and shadows numberless,
 Singest of summer in full-throated ease.

O, for a draught of vintage! that hath been
Cool'd a long age in the deep-delved earth,
 Tasting of Flora and the country green,
Dance, and Provençal song, and sunburnt mirth!
 O for a beaker full of the warm South,
 Full of the true, the blushful Hippocrene,
 With beaded bubbles winking at the brim,
 And purple-stained mouth;
That I might drink, and leave the world unseen,
 And with thee fade away into the forest dim:

John Keats, 1795-1821

Summer Swarm

THE cottage faced south and, in summer, the window and door stood open all day to the sunshine. When the children from the end house passed close by her doorway, as they had to do every time they went beyond their own garden, they would pause a moment to listen to Queenie's old sheep's-head clock ticking.

There was no other sound; for, after she had finished her housework, Queenie was never indoors while the sun shone. If the children had a message for her, they were told to go round to the beehives, and there they would find her, sitting on a low stool with her lace-pillow on her lap, sometimes working and sometimes dozing with her lilac sunbonnet drawn down over her face to shield it from the sun.

Every fine day, throughout the summer, she sat there 'watching the bees'. She was combining duty and pleasure, for, if they swarmed, she was making sure of not losing the swarm; and, if they did not, it was still, as she said, 'a trate' to sit there, feeling the warmth of the sun, smelling the flowers, and watching 'the craturs' go in and out of the hives.

When, at last, the long-looked-for swarm rose into the air, Queenie would seize her coal shovel and iron spoon and follow it over cabbage beds and down pea-stick alleys, her own or, if necessary, other people's, tanging the spoon on the shovel: *Tang-tang-tangety-tang!*

She said it was the law that, if they were not tanged, and they settled beyond her own garden bounds, she would have no further claim to them. Where they settled, they belonged. That would have been a serious loss, especially in early summer, for, as she reminded the children:

> A swarm in May's worth a rick of hay;
>
> And a swarm in June's worth a silver spoon;

while

> A swarm in July isn't worth a fly.

So she would follow and leave her shovel to mark her claim, then go back home for the straw skep and her long, green veil and sheepskin gloves to protect her face and hands while she hived her swarm.

From *Larkrise to Candleford* by Flora Thompson, 1876-1947

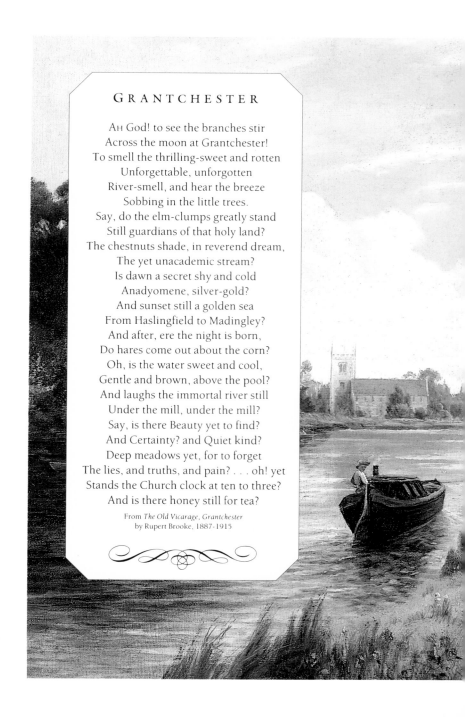

GRANTCHESTER

Ah God! to see the branches stir
Across the moon at Grantchester!
To smell the thrilling-sweet and rotten
Unforgettable, unforgotten
River-smell, and hear the breeze
Sobbing in the little trees.
Say, do the elm-clumps greatly stand
Still guardians of that holy land?
The chestnuts shade, in reverend dream,
The yet unacademic stream?
Is dawn a secret shy and cold
Anadyomene, silver-gold?
And sunset still a golden sea
From Haslingfield to Madingley?
And after, ere the night is born,
Do hares come out about the corn?
Oh, is the water sweet and cool,
Gentle and brown, above the pool?
And laughs the immortal river still
Under the mill, under the mill?
Say, is there Beauty yet to find?
And Certainty? and Quiet kind?
Deep meadows yet, for to forget
The lies, and truths, and pain? . . . oh! yet
Stands the Church clock at ten to three?
And is there honey still for tea?

From *The Old Vicarage, Grantchester*
by Rupert Brooke, 1887-1915

TITANIA'S BOWER

I KNOW a bank where the wild thyme blows,
Where oxlips and the nodding violet grows,
Quite over-canopied with luscious woodbine,
With sweet musk-roses, and with eglantine;
There sleeps Titania sometime of the night,
Lull'd in these flowers with dances and delight;
And there the snake throws her enamell'd skin,
Weed wide enough to wrap a fairy in;
And with the juice of this I'll streak her eyes,
And make her full of hateful fantasies.
Take thou some of it, and seek through this grove:
A sweet Athenian lady is in love
With a disdainful youth; anoint his eyes;
But do it when the next thing he espies
May be the lady. Thou shalt know the man
By the Athenian garments he hath on.
Effect it with some care, that he may prove
More fond on her than she upon her love.
And look thou meet me ere the first cock crow.

From *A Midsummer Night's Dream*
by William Shakespeare, 1564-1616

SONG

How sweet I roam'd from field to field,
   And tasted all the summer's pride,
    'Till I the prince of love beheld,
    Who in the sunny beams did glide!

He shew'd me lilies for my hair,
   And blushing roses for my brow;
   He led me through his gardens fair,
    Where all his golden pleasures grow.

With sweet May dews my wings were we
   And Phœbus fir'd my vocal rage;
   He caught me in his silken net,
    And shut me in his golden cage.

He loves to sit and hear me sing,
Then, laughing, sports and plays with me
   Then stretches out my golden wing,
    And mocks my loss of liberty.

William Blake, 1757-1827

THE LONGEST DAY

LET us quit the leafy arbour,
And the torrent murmuring by;
For the sun is in his harbour,
Weary of the open sky.

Evening now unbinds the fetters
Fashioned by the glowing light;
All that breathe are thankful debtors
To the harbinger of night.

Yet by some grave thoughts attended
Eve renews her calm career;
For the day that now is ended
Is the longest of the year.

Dora! sport, as now thou sportest,
On this platform, light and free;
Take they bliss, while longest, shortest,
Are indifferent to thee!

William Wordsworth, 1770-1850

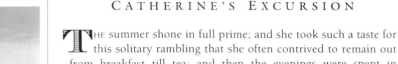

CATHERINE'S EXCURSION

THE summer shone in full prime; and she took such a taste for this solitary rambling that she often contrived to remain out from breakfast till tea; and then the evenings were spent in recounting her fanciful tales. I did not fear her breaking bounds; because the gates were generally locked, and I thought she would scarcely venture forth alone, if they had stood wide open. Unluckily, my confidence proved misplaced. Catherine came to me, one morning, at eight o'clock, and said she was that day an Arabian merchant, going to cross the Desert with his caravan; and I must give her plenty of provision for herself and beasts: a horse, and three camels, personated by a large hound and a couple of pointers. I got together good store of dainties, and slung them in a basket on one side of the saddle; and she sprang up as gay as a fairy, sheltered by her wide-brimmed hat and gauze veil from the July sun, and trotted off with a merry laugh, mocking my cautious counsel to avoid galloping, and come back early. The naughty thing never made her appearance at tea. One traveller, the hound, being an old dog and fond of its ease, returned; but neither Cathy, nor the pony, nor the two pointers were visible in any direction: I despatched emissaries down this path, and that path, and at last went wandering in search of her myself. There was a labourer working at a fence round a plantation, on the borders of the grounds. I inquired of him if he had seen our young lady.

'I saw her at morn,' he replied: 'she would have me to cut her a hazel switch, and then she leapt her Galloway over the hedge yonder, where it is lowest, and galloped out of sight.'

From *Wuthering Heights* by Emily Brontë, 1815-1848

SUMMER RETREAT

THE train for Marmion left Boston at four o'clock in the afternoon, and rambled fitfully toward the southern cape, while the shadows grew long in the stony pastures and the slanting light gilded the straggling, shabby woods, and painted the ponds and marshes with yellow gleams. The ripeness of summer lay upon the land, and yet there was nothing in the country Basil Ransom traversed that seemed susceptible of maturity; nothing but the apples in the little tough, dense orchards, which gave a suggestion of sour fruition here and there, and the tall, bright golden-rod at the bottom of the bare stone dykes. There were no fields of yellow grain; only here and there a crop of brown hay. But there was a kind of soft scrubbiness in the landscape, and a sweetness begotten of low horizons, of mild air, with a possibility of summer haze, of unregarded inlets where on August mornings the water must be brightly blue. Ransom had heard that the Cape was the Italy, so to speak, of Massachusetts; it had been described to him as the drowsy Cape, the languid Cape, the Cape not of storms, but of eternal peace.

From *The Bostonians* by Henry James, 1843-1916

A Rainy Season

August 15th – Cold, cloudy, windy, wet. Here we are, in the midst of the dog-days, clustering merrily round the warm hearth like so many crickets, instead of chirruping in the green fields like that other merry insect the grasshopper; shivering under the influence of the *Jupiter Pluvius* of England, the watery St. Swithin; peering at that scarce personage the sun, when he happens to make his appearance, as intently as astronomers look after a comet, or the common people stare at a balloon; exclaiming against the cold weather, just as we used to exclaim against the warm. 'What a change from last year!' is the first sentence you hear, go where you may. . . .

It keeps us within, to be sure, rather more than is quite agreeable; but then we are at least awake and alive there, and the world out of doors is so much the pleasanter when we can get abroad. Everything does well, except those fastidious bipeds, men and women; corn ripens, grass grows, fruit is plentiful; there is no lack of birds to eat it, and there has not been such a wasp-season these dozen years. My garden wants no watering, and is more beautiful than ever, beating my old rival in that primitive art, the pretty wife of the little mason, out and out. Measured with mine, her flowers are naught. Look at those hollyhocks, like pyramids of roses; those garlands of the convolvulus major of all colours, hanging around that tall pole, like the wreathy hop-bine; those magnificent dusky cloves, breathing of the Spice Islands; those flaunting double dahlias; those splendid scarlet geraniums, and those fierce and warlike flowers the tiger-lilies. Oh, how beautiful they are! Besides, the weather clears sometimes – it has cleared this evening; and here are we, after a merry walk up the hill, almost as quick as in the winter, bounding lightly along the bright green turf of the pleasant common, enticed by the gay shouts of a dozen clear young voices, to linger awhile, and see the boys play at cricket.

From *Our Village* by Mary Russell Mitford, 1787-1855

GOBLIN MARKET

MORNING and evening
Maids heard the goblins cry:
"Come buy our orchard fruits,
Come buy, come buy:
Apples and quinces,
Lemons and oranges,
Plump unpecked cherries,
Melons and raspberries,
Bloom-down-cheeked peaches,
Swart-headed mulberries,
Wild free-born cranberries,
Crab-apples, dewberries,
Pine-apples, blackberries,
Apricots, strawberries:–
All ripe together
In summer weather, –
Morns that pass by,
Fair eves that fly;
Come buy, come buy:
Our grapes fresh from the vine,
Pomegranates full and fine,
Dates and sharp bullaces,
Rare pears and greengages,
Damsons and bilberries,
Taste them and try:
Currants and gooseberries,
Bright-fire-like barberries,
Figs to fill your mouth,
Citrons from the South,
Sweet to tongue and sound to eye;
Come buy, come buy."

Christina Rossetti , 1830-1894

LITTLE IDA'S FLOWERS

'My flowers are quite faded,' said little Ida. 'Only yesterday evening they were so pretty, and now they are all drooping! What can be the reason of it?' asked she of the student who was sitting on the sofa, and who was a great favourite with her, because he used to tell her stories, and cut out all sorts of pretty things for her in paper – such as hearts with little ladies dancing in them, flowers, high castles with open doors, etc. 'Why do these flowers look so deplorable?' asked she again, showing him a bouquet of faded flowers.

'Do you not know?' replied the student. 'Your flowers went to a ball last night, and are tired; that is why they all hang their heads.'

'Surely flowers cannot dance!' exclaimed little Ida.

'Of course they can dance! When it is dark, and we have all gone to bed, they jump about as merrily as possible. They have a ball almost every night.'

'May children go to the ball, too?' asked Ida.

'Yes,' said the student; 'daisies and lilies of the valley.'

'And where do the prettiest flowers dance?'

'Have you never been in the large garden in front of the King's beautiful summer palace – the garden so full of flowers? Surely you remember the swans that come swimming up to you, when you throw them crumbs of bread? There you may imagine they have splendid balls.'

From *Fairy Tales* by Hans Christian Andersen, 1805-1875

Autumn

Autumn in felted slipper shuffles on,
Muted yet fiery, — Autumn's character.
Brown as a monk yet flaring as a whore,
And in the distance blue as Raphael's robe
Tender around the Virgin.
Blue the smoke
Drifting across brown woods; but in the garden
Maples are garish, and surprising leaves
Make sudden fires with sudden crests of flame
Where the sun hits them; in the deep-cut leaf
Of peony, like a mediaeval axe
Of rusty iron; fervour of azalea
Whose dying days repeat her June of flower;
In Sargent's cherry, upright as a torch
Till ravelled sideways by the wind to stream
Disorderly, and strew the mint of sparks
In coins of pointed metal, cooling down;
And that true child of Fall, whose morbid fruit
Ripens, with walnuts, only in November,
The Medlar lying brown across the thatch;
Rough elbows of rough branches, russet fruit
So blet it's worth no more than sleepy pear,
But in its motley pink and yellow leaf
A harlequin that some may overlook
Nor ever think to break and set within
A vase of bronze against a wall of oak,
With Red-hot Poker, Autumn's final torch.

Vita Sackville-West, 1892-1962

ENDYMION

So, she was gently glad to see him laid
Under her favourite bower's quiet shade,
On her own couch, new made of flower leaves,
Dried carefully on the cooler side of sheaves
When last the sun his autumn tresses shook,
And the tann'd harvesters rich armfuls took.
Soon was he quieted to slumbrous rest:
But, ere it crept upon him, he had prest
Peona's busy hand against his lips,
And still, a-sleeping, held her finger-tips
In tender pressure. And as a willow keeps
A patient watch over the stream that creeps
Windingly by it, so the quiet maid
Held her in peace: so that a whispering blade
Of grass, a wailful gnat, a bee bustling
Down in the blue-bells, or a wren light rustling
Among sere leaves and twigs, might all be heard.

O magic sleep! O comfortable bird,
That broodest o'er the troubled sea of the mind
Till it is hush'd and smooth! O unconfin'd
Restraint! imprisoned liberty! great key
To golden palaces, strange minstrelsy,
Fountains grotesque, new trees, bespangled caves,
Echoing grottoes, full of tumbling waves
And moonlight; aye, to all the mazy world
Of silvery enchantment! – who, upfurl'd
Beneath thy drowsy wing a triple hour,
But renovates and lives? – Thus, in the bower,
Endymion was calm'd to life again.

John Keats, 1795-1821

AUTUMN FIRES

IN the other gardens
And all up the vale,
From the autumn bonfires
See the smoke trail!

Pleasant summer over
And all the summer flowers,
The red fire blazes,
The grey smoke towers.

Sing a song of seasons!
Something bright in all!
Flowers in the summer,
Fires in the fall!

Robert Louis Stevenson, 1850-1894

HARVEST TIME

Iɴ the fields where the harvest had begun all was bustle and activity. At that time the mechanical reaper with long, red, revolving arms like windmill sails had already appeared in the locality; but it was looked upon by the men as an auxiliary, a farmers' toy; the scythe still did most of the work and they did not dream it would ever be superseded. So while the red sails revolved in one field and the youth on the driver's seat of the machine called cheerily to his horses and women followed behind to bind the corn into sheaves, in the next field a band of men would be whetting their scythes and mowing by hand as their fathers had done before them.

With no idea that they were at the end of a long tradition, they still kept up the old country custom of choosing as their leader the tallest and most highly skilled man amongst them, who was then called 'King of the Mowers'. For several harvests in the 'eighties they were led by the man known as Boamer. He had served in the Army and was still a fine, well-set-up young fellow with flashing white teeth and a skin darkened by fiercer than English suns.

With a wreath of poppies and green bindweed trails around his wide, rush-plaited hat, he led the band down the swathes as they mowed and decreed when and for how long they should halt for 'a breather' and what drinks should be had from the yellow stone jar they kept under the hedge in a shady corner of the field. They did not rest often or long; for every morning they set themselves to accomplish an amount of work in the day that they knew would tax all their powers till long after sunset. 'Set yourself more than you can do and you'll do it' was one of their maxims, and some of their feats in the harvest field astonished themselves as well as the onlooker.

From *Lark Rise to Candleford* by Flora Thompson, 1876-1947

A UTUMN S TARS

WHEN they came in they sat beside the fire in the oak drawing-room, and Darrow noticed how delicately her head stood out against the sombre panelling, and mused on the enjoyment there would always be in the mere fact of watching her hands as they moved about among the tea-things . . .

They dined late, and facing her across the table, with its low lights and flowers, he felt an extraordinary pleasure in seeing her again in evening dress, and in letting his eyes dwell on the proud shy set of her head, the way her dark hair clasped it, and the girlish thinness of her neck above the slight swell of the breast. His imagination was struck by the quality of reticence in her beauty. She suggested a fine portrait kept down to a few tones, or a Greek vase on which the play of light is the only pattern.

After dinner they went out on the terrace for a look at the moon-misted park. Through the crepuscular whiteness the trees hung in blotted masses. Below the terrace, the garden drew its dark diagrams between statues that stood like muffled conspirators on the edge of the shadow. Farther off, the meadows unrolled a silver-shot tissue to the mantling of mist above the river; and the autumn stars trembled overhead like their own reflections seen in the water.

From *The Reef* by Edith Wharton, 1862-1937

SONNET

THAT time of year thou may'st in me behold
When yellow leaves, or none, or few, do hang
Upon those boughs which shake against the cold –
Bare ruin'd choirs where late the sweet birds sang.
In me thou see'st the twilight of such day
As after Sunset fadeth in the West,
Which by and by black night doth take away,
Death's second self, that seals up all in rest.
In me thou see'st the glowing of such fire
That on the ashes of his youth doth lie,
As the death-bed whereon it must expire,
Consumed with that which it was nourish'd by.
This thou perceiv'st, which makes thy love more strong
To love that well which thou must leave ere long.

William Shakespeare, 1564-1616

BAVARIAN GENTIANS

NOT every man has gentians in his house
in Soft September, at slow, Sad Michaelmas.

Bavarian gentians, big and dark, only dark
darkening the day-time torch-like with the smoking blueness of Pluto's gloom,
ribbed and torch-like, with their blaze of darkness spread blue
down flattening into points, flattened under the sweep of white day
torch-flower of the blue-smoking darkness, Pluto's dark-blue daze,
black lamps from the halls of Dis, burning dark blue,
giving off darkness, blue darkness, as Demeter's pale lamps give off light,
lead me then, lead me the way.

Reach me a gentian, give me a torch
let me guide myself with the blue, forked torch of this flower
down the darker and darker stairs, where blue is darkened on blueness.
Even where Persephone goes, just now, from the frosted September
to the sightless realm where darkness is awake upon the dark
and Persephone herself is but a voice
or a darkness invisible enfolded in the deeper dark
of the arms of Plutonic, and pierced with the passion of dense gloom,
among the splendour of torches of darkness, shedding darkness on the lost
bride and her groom.

D. H. Lawrence, 1885-1930

MICHAELMAS DAISIES

THE early days of October bring with them the best bloom of the Michaelmas Daisies, the many beautiful garden kinds of the perennial Asters. They have, as they well deserve to have, a garden to themselves. Passing along the wide path in front of the big flower border, and through the pergola that forms its continuation, with eye and brain full of rich, warm colouring of flower and leaf, it is a delightful surprise to pass through the pergola's last right-hand opening, and to come suddenly upon the Michaelmas Daisy garden in full beauty. Its clean, fresh, pure colouring, of pale and dark lilac, strong purple, and pure white, among masses of pale-green foliage, forms a contrast almost startling after the warm colouring of nearly everything else; and the sight of a region where the flowers are fresh and newly opened, and in glad spring-like profusion, when all else is on the verge of death and decay, gives an impression of satisfying refreshment that is hardly to be equalled throughout the year.

From *Wood and Garden* by Gertrude Jekyll, 1843-1932

GATHERING LEAVES

SPADES take up leaves
No better than spoons,
And bags full of leaves
Are light as balloons.

I make a great noise
Of rustling all day
Like a rabbit and deer
Running away.

But the mountains I raise
Elude my embrace,
Flowing over my arms
And into my face.

I may load and unload
Again and again
Till I fill the whole shed,
And what have I then?

Next to nothing for weight;
And since they grew duller
From contact with earth,
Next to nothing for color.

Next to nothing for use.
But a crop is a crop,
And who's to say where
The harvest shall stop?

Robert Frost, 1874-1963

APPLE HARVEST

Our Apple harvest has been over for nearly a fortnight; but how pleasant the orchard was while it lasted, and how pleasant the seat in the corner by the Limes, whence we see the distant spire on the green wooded slopes. The grey, gnarled old Apple-trees have, for the most part, done well. The Ribston Pippins are especially fine, and so is an apple, which we believe to be the King of the Pippins. On the other hand, we have some poor and worthless sorts – probably local varieties, – which no pomologist, however able and obliging, would undertake to name. One of the prettiest of Apples – and one of the best, too – is the Delaware. It has an orange-red colour, and reminds one almost of an Orange as it hangs upon the tree. It has a crisp, delicious flavour, but requires to be eaten as soon as it is ripe, for otherwise it soon gets mealy. Indeed all eating apples, with but few exceptions, are best when freshly gathered, or, better still, when, on some clear soft day, they have just fallen on the grass, and lie there, warmed by the rays of the autumn sun.

From *A Year in a Lancashire Garden* by Henry A. Bright, 1891

WENLOCK EDGE

On Wenlock Edge the wood's in trouble;
His forest fleece the Wrekin heaves;
The gale, it plies the saplings double,
And thick on Severn snow the leaves.

'Twould blow like this through holt and hanger
When Uricon the city stood:
'Tis the old wind in the old anger,
But then it threshed another wood.

Then, 'twas before my time, the Roman
At yonder heaving hill would stare:
The blood that warms an English yoeman,
The thoughts that hurt him, they were there.

There, like the wind through woods in riot,
Through him the gale of life blew high;
The tree of man was never quiet:
Then 'twas the Roman, now 'tis I.

The gale, it plies the saplings double,
It blows so hard, 'twill soon be gone:
To-day the Roman and his trouble
Are ashed under Uricon.

A. E. Houseman, 1859-1936

To Autumn

Season of mists and mellow fruitfulness,
　　Close bosom-friend of the maturing sun;
　　Conspiring with him how to load and bless
With fruit the vines that round the thatch-eves run;
　　To bend with apples the moss'd cottage-trees,
　　　And fill all fruit with ripeness to the core;
　　To swell the gourd, and plump the hazel shells
　　　With a sweet kernel; to set budding more,
　　　And still more, later flowers for the bees,
　　Until they think warm days will never cease,
For Summer has o'er-brimm'd their clammy cells.

Who hath not seen thee oft amid thy store?
　　Sometimes whoever seeks abroad may find
　　Thee sitting careless on a granary floor,
　　Thy hair soft-lifted by winnowing wind;
　　Or on a half-reap'd furrow sound asleep,
　　Drows'd with the fume of poppies, while thy hook
　　Spares the next swath and all its twined flowers:
　　And sometimes like a gleaner thou dost keep
　　　Steady thy laden head across a brook;
　　　Or by a cyder-press, with patient look,
　　Thou watchest the last oozings hours by hours.

Where are the songs of Spring? Ay, where are they?
　　Think not of them, thou hast thy music too, —
　　While barred clouds bloom the soft-dying day,
　　And touch the stubble-plains with rosy hue;
　　Then in a wailful choir the small gnats mourn
　　　Among the river sallows, borne aloft
　　　Or sinking as the light wind lives or dies;
　　And full-grown lambs loud bleat from hilly bourn;
　　Hedge-crickets sing; and now with treble soft
　　　The red-breast whistles from a garden-croft;
　　And gathering swallows twitter in the skies.

John Keats, 1795-1821

WINTER

Blow, blow thou winter wind,

Thou art not so unkind

As man's ingratitude;

Thy tooth is not so keen,

Because thou art not seen,

Although thy breath be rude.

William Shakespeare

WINTER-TIME

LATE lies the wintry sun a-bed,
A frosty, fiery sleepy-head;
Blinks but an hour or two; and then,
A blood-red orange, sets again.

Before the stars have left the skies,
At morning in the dark I rise;
And shivering in my nakedness,
By the cold candle, bathe and dress.

Close by the jolly fire I sit
To warm my frozen bones a bit;
Or with a reindeer-sled, explore
The colder countries round the door.

When to go out, my nurse doth wrap
Me in my comforter and cap:
The cold wind burns my face, and blows
Its frosty pepper up my nose.

Black are my steps on silver sod;
Thick blows my frosty breath abroad;
And trees and house, and hill and lake,
Are frosted like a wedding-cake.

Robert Louis Stevenson, 1850-1894

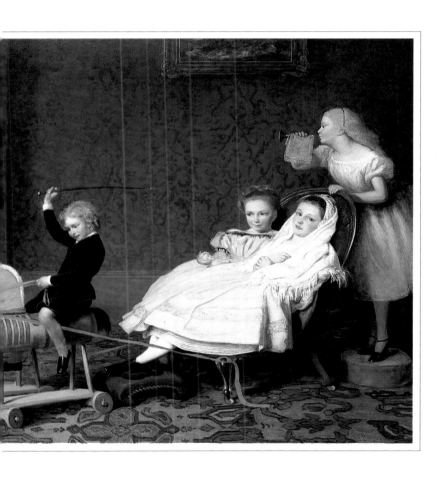

A Frosty Morning

On a frosty morning with a little February sun, Clifford and Connie went for a walk across the park to the wood. That is Clifford chuffed in his motor-chair, and Connie walked beside him.

The hard air was still sulphurous, but they were both used to it. Round the near horizon went the haze, opalescent with frost and smoke, and on the top lay the small blue sky; so that it was like being inside an enclosure, always inside. Life always a dream or a frenzy, inside an enclosure.

The sheep coughed in the rough, sere grass of the park where frost lay bluish in the sockets of the tufts. Across the park ran a path to the wood-gate, a fine ribbon of pink. Clifford had had it newly gravelled with sifted gravel from the pit-bank. When the rock and refuse of the underworld had burned and given off its sulphur, it turned bright pink, shrimp-coloured on dry days, darker, crab-coloured on wet. Now it was pale shrimp-colour, with a bluish-white hoar of frost. It always pleased Connie, this underfoot of sifted, bright pink. It's an ill wind that brings nobody good.

Clifford steered cautiously down the slope of the knoll from the hall, and Connie kept her hand on the chair. In front lay the wood, the hazel thicket nearest, the purplish density of oaks beyond. From the wood's edge rabbits bobbed and nibbled. Rooks suddenly rose in a black train, and went trailing off over the little sky.

Connie opened the wood-gate, and Clifford puffed slowly through into the broad riding that ran up an incline between the clean-whipped thickets of the hazel. The wood was a remnant of the great forest where Robin Hood hunted, and this riding was an old, old thoroughfare coming across country. But now, of course, it was only a riding through the private wood. The road from Mansfield swerved round to the north.

From *Lady Chatterley's Lover* by D. H. Lawrence, 1885-1930

The Eve Of St. Agnes

St. Agnes' Eve – Ah, bitter chill it was!
The owl, for all his feathers, was a-cold;
The hare limp'd trembling through the frozen grass,
And silent was the flock in woolly fold:
Numb were the Beadsman's fingers, while he told
His rosary, and while his frosted breath,
Like pious incense from a censer old,
Seem'd taking flight for heaven, without a death,
Past the sweet Virgin's picture, while his prayer he saith.

His prayer he saith, this patient, holy man;
Then takes his lamp, and riseth from his knees,
And back returneth, meagre, barefoot, wan,
Along the chapel aisle by slow degrees:
The sculptur'd dead, on each side, seem to freeze,
Emprison'd in black purgatorial rails:
Knights, ladies, praying in dumb orat'ries,
He passeth by: and his weak spirit fails
To think how they may ache in icy hoods and mails.

Northward he turneth through a little door,
And scarce three steps, ere Music's golden tongue
Flatter'd to tears this aged man and poor;
But no – already had his deathbell rung:
The joys of all his life were said and sung:
His was harsh penance on St. Agnes' Eve:
Another way he went, and soon among
Rough ashes he sat for his soul's reprieve,
And all night kept awake, for sinners' sake to grieve.

John Keats, 1795-1821

SONNET

How like a Winter hath my absence been
From thee, the pleasure of the fleeting year!
What freezings have I felt, what dark days seen,
What old December's bareness everywhere!
And yet this time removed was summer's time;
The teeming Autumn, big with rich increase,
Bearing the wanton burden of the prime
Like widow'd wombs after their Lord's decease:
Yet this abundant issue seem'd to me
But hope of orphans and unfather'd fruit;
For Summer and his pleasures wait on thee,
And, thou away, the very birds are mute:
Or if they sing, 'tis with so dull a cheer
That leaves look pale, dreading the Winter's near.

William Shakespeare, 1564-1616

FROM THE WINDOW

THE western windows of Olive's drawing-room, looking over the water, took in the red sunsets of winter; the long, low bridge that crawled, on its staggering posts, across the Charles; the casual patches of ice and snow; the desolate suburban horizons, peeled and made bald by the rigour of the season; the general hard, cold void of the prospect; the extrusion, at Charlestown, at Cambridge, of a few chimneys and steeples, straight, sordid tubes of factories and engine-shops, or spare, heavenward finger of the New England meeting-house. There was something inexorable in the poverty of the scene, shameful in the meanness of its details, which gave a collective impression of boards and tin and frozen earth, sheds and rotting piles. . . .

Verena thought such a view lovely, and she was by no means without excuse when, as the afternoon closed, the ugly picture was tinted with a clear, cold rosiness. The air, in its windless chill, seemed to tinkle like a crystal, the faintest gradations of tone were perceptible in the sky, the west became deep and delicate, everything grew doubly distinct before taking on the dimness of evening. There were pink flushes on snow, 'tender' reflections in patches of stiffened marsh, sounds of car-bells, no longer vulgar, but almost silvery, on the long bridge, lonely outlines of distant dusky undulations against the fading glow. These agreeable effects used to light up that end of the drawing-room, and Olive often sat at the window with her companion before it was time for the lamp. They admired the sunsets, they rejoiced in the ruddy spots projected upon the parlour-wall, they followed the darkening perspective in fanciful excursions. They watched the stellar points come out at last in a colder heaven, and then, shuddering a little, arm in arm, they turned away, with a sense that the winter night was even more cruel than the tyranny of men – turned back to drawn curtains and brighter fire and a glittering tea-tray and more and more talk about the long martydom of women, a subject as to which Olive was inexhaustable and really most interesting.

From *The Bostonians* by Henry James, 1843-1916

A COLD CHRISTENING

Septuagesima Sunday, St. Valentine's Eve

P REACHED at Clyro in the morning (Matthew xiv, 30). Very few people in Church, the weather fearful, violent deadly E. wind and the hardest frost we have had yet. Went to Bettws in the afternoon wrapped in two waistcoats, two coats, a muffler and a mackintosh, and was not at all too warm. Heard the Chapel bell pealing strongly for the second time since I have been here and when I got to the Chapel my beard moustaches and whiskers were so stiff with ice that I could hardly open my mouth and my beard was frozen on to my mackintosh. There was a large christening party from Llwyn Gwilym. The baby was baptized in ice which was broken and swimming about in the Font.

From *The Diary of the Reverend Frances Kilvert*, 1870

Dancing With The Fezziwigs

I<small>N</small> came a fiddler with a music-book, and went up to the lofty
desk, and made an orchestra of it, and tuned like fifty
stomach-aches. In came Mrs. Fezziwig, one vast substantial smile.
In came the three Miss Fezziwigs, beaming and lovable. In came
the six young followers whose hearts they broke. In came all the
young men and women employed in the business. In came the

housemaid, with her cousin, the baker. In came the cook, with her brother's particular friend, the milkman. In came the boy from over the way, who was suspected of not having board enough from his master; trying to hide himself behind the girl from next door but one, who was proved to have had her ears pulled by her Mistress. In they all came, one after another; some shyly, some boldly, some gracefully, some awkwardly, some pushing, some pulling; in they all came, anyhow and everyhow. Away they all went, twenty couple at once, hands half round and back again the other way; down the middle and up again; round and round in various stages of affectionate grouping; old top couple always turning up in the wrong place; new top couple starting off again, as soon as they got there; all top couples at last, and not a bottom one to help them. When this result was brought about, old Fezziwig, clapping his hands to stop the dance, cried out, 'Well done!' and the fiddler plunged his hot face into a pot of porter, especially provided for that purpose. But scorning rest upon his reappearance, he instantly began again, though there were no dancers yet, as if the other fiddler had been carried home, exhausted, on a shutter; and he were a bran-new man resolved to beat him out of sight, or perish.

There were more dances, and there were forfeits, and more dances, and there was cake, and there was negus, and there was a great piece of Cold Roast, and there was a great piece of Cold, Boiled, and there were mince pies, and plenty of beer. But the great effect of the evening came after the Roast and Boiled, when the fiddler (an artful dog, mind! The sort of man who knew his business better than you or I could have told it him!) struck up 'Sir Roger de Coverley.' Then old Fezziwig stood out to dance with Mrs. Fezziwig. Top couple, too; with a good stiff piece of work cut out for them; three or four and twenty pair of partners; people who were not to be trifled with; people who *would* dance, and had no notion of walking.

From *A Christmas Carol* by Charles Dickens, 1812-1870

SONG

WHEN icicles hang by the wall,
And Dick the shepherd blows his nail.
And Tom bears logs into the hall,
And milk comes frozen home in pail,
When blood is nipp'd and ways be foul,
Then nightly sings the staring owl,
To-whit!
To-who! – a merry note,
While greasy Joan doth keel the pot.

When all aloud the wind doth blow,
And coughing drowns the parson's saw,
And birds sit brooding in the snow,
And Marian's nose looks red and raw,
When roasted crabs hiss in the bowl,
Then nightly sings the staring owl,
To-whit!
To-who! – a merry note,
While greasy Joan doth keel the pot.

William Shakespeare, 1564-1616

PICTURE-BOOKS
IN WINTER

SUMMER fading, winter comes –
Frosty mornings, tingling thumbs,
Window robins, winter rooks,
And the picture story-books.

Water now is turned to stone
Nurse and I can walk upon;
Still we find the flowing brooks
In the picture story-books.

All the pretty things put by,
Wait upon the children's eye,
Sheep and shepherds, trees and crooks,
In the picture story-books.

We may see how all things are,
Seas and cities, near and far,
And the flying fairies' looks,
In the picture story-books.

How am I to sing your praise,
Happy chimney-corner days,
Sitting safe in nursery nooks,
Reading picture story-books?

Robert Louis Stevenson, 1850-1894

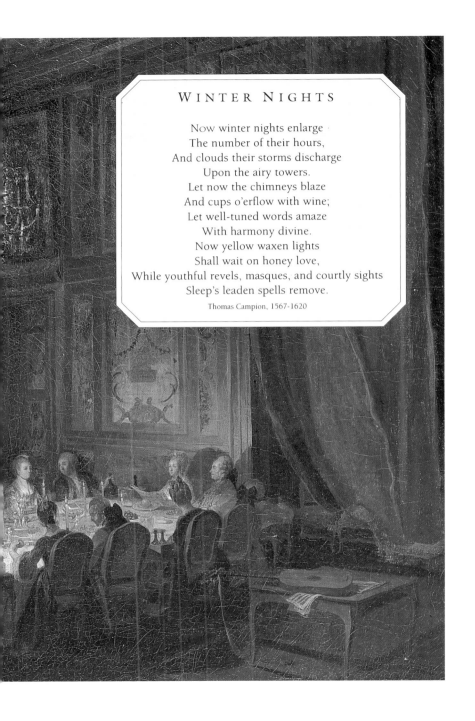

WINTER NIGHTS

Now winter nights enlarge
The number of their hours,
And clouds their storms discharge
Upon the airy towers.
Let now the chimneys blaze
And cups o'erflow with wine;
Let well-tuned words amaze
With harmony divine.
Now yellow waxen lights
Shall wait on honey love,
While youthful revels, masques, and courtly sights
Sleep's leaden spells remove.

Thomas Campion, 1567-1620

WINTER FANCIES

WINTER without
And warmth within;
The winds may shout
And the storm begin;
The snows may pack
At the window-pane,
And the skies grow black,
And the sun remain
Hidden away
The livelong day –
But here – in here is the warmth of May!

Swoop your spitefullest
Up the flue,
Wild Winds – do!
What in the world do I care for you?

O delightfullest
Weather of all,
Howl and squall,
And shake the trees till the last leaves fall!

James Whitcomb Riley, 1849-1916

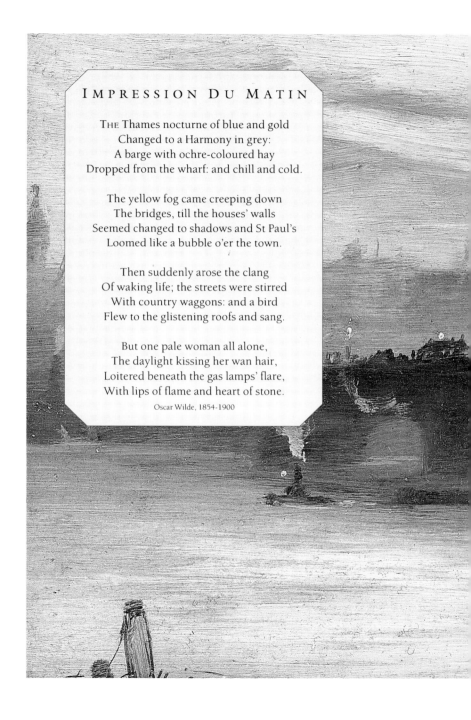

IMPRESSION DU MATIN

THE Thames nocturne of blue and gold
Changed to a Harmony in grey:
A barge with ochre-coloured hay
Dropped from the wharf: and chill and cold.

The yellow fog came creeping down
The bridges, till the houses' walls
Seemed changed to shadows and St Paul's
Loomed like a bubble o'er the town.

Then suddenly arose the clang
Of waking life; the streets were stirred
With country waggons: and a bird
Flew to the glistening roofs and sang.

But one pale woman all alone,
The daylight kissing her wan hair,
Loitered beneath the gas lamps' flare,
With lips of flame and heart of stone.

Oscar Wilde, 1854-1900

PENHALIGON'S GARDENIA

The heady, waxy scent of Penhaligon's 'Gardenia' comes from the hot gardens by the Mediterranean sea. It is a lingering evocative fragrance, reminiscent of exotic days and balmy nights.

For more information about Penhaligon's perfumes,
or a sample of Penhaligon's 'Gardenia', please telephone
London 0181-880 2050 (or from America, 011-44-181-880-2050)
or write to:

PENHALIGON'S
41 Wellington Street
Covent Garden
London WC2

ACKNOWLEDGEMENTS

In order of appearance.
All material supplied by Bridgeman Art Library, London, unless
otherwise indicated.

Anthony Sandys/University of Dundee; Sir George Clausen/Fine
Arts Society/Private Collection; Alexander Mann/Whitford &
Hughes; Daniel Hernandez/Whitford & Hughes; Paul Gustaf
Fischer/Amell Fine Art, Stockholm/Courtesy Medici Society;
Edmund Blair Leighton/Fine Art Photographic Archive; Herman
Richir/Bonham's, London; Arthur Hughes/Forbes Magazine
Collection, New York; Harry Foskey/Fine Art Photographic
Archive; Henry Ryland/Sotheby's, London/Private Collection;
George Dunlop Leslie/Royal Academy of Arts, London; Elizabeth
Sonrel/Whitford & Hughes; Joseph Marius Avy/Musee de Petit
Palais, Paris; Ester Borough Johnson/Whitford & Hughes; Ernest
Rocher/Whitford & Hughes; Dante Gabriel Rossetti/Guildhall Art
Gallery, London; Lucius Rossi/Fine Art Photographic Archive;
James N Lee/Fine Art Photographic Archive; Eleanor Fortesque-
Brickdale/City of Bristol Museum & Art Gallery; Cassels Book
Birds/Private Collection; Leopold Rivers/Fine Art Photographic
Archive; Allan Mell/Fine Art Photographic Archive; Edward Robert
Hughes/Fine Art Photographic Archive; Evelyn De Morgan/De
Morgan Foundation; Tom Lloyd/Chris Beetles Ltd; Henry
H Emmerson/Fine Art Photographic Archive; Peter Severin
Kroyer/Skagens Museum, Denmark; A Templeuve/Fine Art
Photographic Archive; Edward Reginald Frampton/Mass Gallery,
London; A J Billinghurst/Private Collection; Leon Giran-Max/Fine
Art Photographic Archive; Alfred de Breanski/Private
Collection/Elgin Court; Sir Frank Dicksee/Fine Art Society,
London; José de Souza Pinto/Musee D'Orsay, Paris; Alexander
Mann/Fine Art Society, London; David Jagger/Private Collection;
G D Ehret/Private Collection; Patrick William Adam/Gavin
Graham Gallery, London; Sir John Everett Millais/Manchester City

Art Gallery; Frederick Daniel Harvey/Fine Art Photographic Archive; J H S Mann/Royal Holloway & Bedford College, Surrey; Dante Gabriel Rossetti/Tate Gallery, London; Edgar Maxence/Whitford & Hughes; William Bramley/Fine Art Photographic Archive; James Jacques Tissot/Private Collection; John Malhuish Strudwick/Roy Miles Fine Paintings, London; John Callcott Horsley/Fine Art Photographic Archive; Wilfred de Glehn/David Messum Galleries, London & Beaconsfield; William Bromley/Fine Art Photographic Archive; Edward Bird/Wolverhampton Art Gallery; Henri Eugene Augustine Le Sidaner/Private Collection; George Harcourt/David Messum Galleries, London & Beaconsfield; Michel Barthelemy Olivier/Chateau de Versailles, Paris; Sir John Everett Millais/Guildhall Art Gallery; George Hyde Pownall/Fine Art Photographic Archive

Jacket: *Proserpine* by Dante Gabriel Rossetti, Tate Gallery, London
Jacket panel: 'Golden Lily' by William Morris, courtesy of Sanderson Ltd./National Trust Photographic Archive

Text Acknowledgements

'The Twenty-Second of February', 1940 from *Country Notes in Wartime* by Vita Sackville-West, reproduced by permission of Curtis Brown Ltd., London

'Autumn' from *The Garden* by Vita Sackville-West © Vita Sackville-West, reproduced by permission of Curtis Brown Ltd., London

Larkrise to Candleford by Flora Thompson (1945) by permission of Oxford University Press

'Gathering Leaves' from *The Poetry of Robert Frost* edited by Edward Connery Latham, © 1923, © 1969 by Holt Reinhart & Winston © 1951 by Robert Frost. Reprinted in the British Commonwealth by permission of Jonathan Cape Ltd. and in the USA with permission of Henry Holt & Co Inc., USA

First published in Great Britain in 1995 by
PAVILION BOOKS LIMITED
26 Upper Ground, London SE1 9PD

Compiled from original volumes:
Morning Glory, 1992, Summer's Cup, 1991
Forest's Robe, 1992, The Winter Garden, 1992

Compilation and Introduction
© Sheila Pickles 1995

A CIP catalogue record for this book is available from the
British Library

Designed by Bernard Higton
and Andrew Barron and Collis Clements Associates
Picture research by Linda Marshall

ISBN 1 85793 471 7

Manufactured in China for Imago

2 4 6 8 10 9 7 5 3 1

This book may be ordered by post direct from the publisher.
Please contact the Marketing Department.
But try your bookshop first.